A JANE AUSTEN

# JOURNAL

*With Notable Quotations from*
**Jane Austen**

**CHRONICLE BOOKS**
SAN FRANCISCO

*Her own*

# THOUGHTS

# REFLECTIONS

*were habitually
her best companions*

*Mansfield Park*

*One's happiness
must in some measure
be always at the*

*mercy*

of

CHANCE

*Sense and Sensibility*

*Her*

*manners were the*

# MIRROR

*of her own*

*modest*

&

*elegant mind*

Henry Crawford, *Mansfield Park*

*Four sides of paper*

*all her delight*

*were insufficient*

*to contain*

*Pride and Prejudice*

*If*
*I loved you*

# LESS

*I might be able*
*to talk about it*

# MORE

Mr. Knightley, *Emma*

*I*

*suppose*

*there may be a*

# HUNDRED

*different ways*

*of being*

*in*

Love Love Love Love Love Love Love Love Love Love Love Love Love Love Love Love Love Love Love Love Love Love Love Love Love Love Love Love Love Love Love Love Love Love Love Love Love Love Love Love Love Love Love Love Love Love Love Love Love Love Love Love Love Love Love Love Love Love Love Love Love Love Love Love Love Love Love Love Love Love Love Love Love Love Love Love Love Love Love Love Love Love Love Love Love Love Love Love Love Love Love

Emma Woodhouse, *Emma*

# I
## DID NOT
## THEN KNOW

*what it was to*

## Love

Willoughby, *Sense and Sensibility*

There could have been

no **2** *hearts* so open,

no tastes so similar,

no feelings

so in

# UNISON

*Persuasion*

*Not*
*keep*
*a*

JOUR

NAL

!

Henry Tilney, *Northanger Abbey*

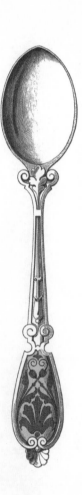

# ONE HALF
# OF THE
# WORLD

*cannot
understand
the pleasures
of the other*

Emma Woodhouse, *Emma*

# *Oh!* write, write.

*Finish it at once.*
*Let there be an end of this suspense.*

FIX  COMMIT ✹ CONDEMN

*yourself.*

Fanny Price, *Mansfield Park*

# Wretched, wretched, mist ke!

Elizabeth Bennet, *Pride and Prejudice*

it is only a

# NOVEL

*Northanger Abbey*

Let
Other pens
Dwell

*on* *guilt and misery*

*Mansfield Park*

There is no

*Charm*

equal to

*tenderness of*

*Heart*

Emma Woodhouse, *Emma*

*These matters*
*are always a*

*secret*

*till it is found out that*
**EVERY BODY**
*knows them*

Mr. Weston, *Emma*

To

# FLATTER

*and follow others,*
*without being flattered*
*and followed in turn,*
*is but a state of*

$$\frac{1}{2}$$

enjoyment

*Persuasion*

# MY

## *Feelings*

### are at present
### in a state of

# DREADFUL

# INDECISION

Marianne Dashwood, *Sense and Sensibility*

**Tell me not that I am *too late***

Captain Wentworth, *Persuasion*

# Pray
## WRITE TO HER
### *if it be only a*

*line*

Henry Crawford, *Mansfield Park*

*Till this*

# MOMENT

# I NEVER KNEW
*myself*

Elizabeth Bennet, *Pride and Prejudice*

*It is well
to have as many*

HOLDS

*upon*

*happiness*

*as possible*

Henry Tilney, *Northanger Abbey*

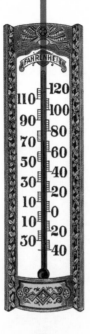

**COURAGE**

*always rises with
every attempt to
intimidate me*

Elizabeth Bennet, *Pride and Prejudice*

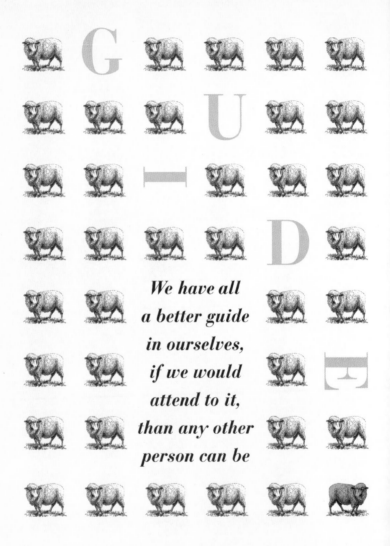

GUIDE

We have all
a better guide
in ourselves,
if we would
attend to it,
than any other
person can be

Fanny Price, *Mansfield Park*

*I cannot be*

# FORCED

*into genius*

&

ELOQUENCE

Edward Ferrars, *Sense and Sensibility*

It is
# A RULE WITH ME,
*that a person who can write a long*

*Letter*

*with ease,*
*cannot*
*write*
*ill*

Caroline Bingley, *Pride and Prejudice*

*I think*
*there cannot be*

T O O

*little said*
*on the*

SUBJECT

Elizabeth Bennet, *Pride and Prejudice*

Her

*happiness*

**was from**

WITHIN

*Persuasion*

*To understand,*

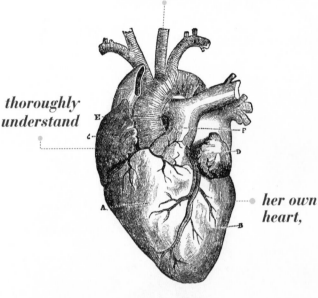

*thoroughly understand*

*her own heart,*

*was the*

# FIRST

*Endeavour*

*Emma*

*It is such a*

# HAPPINESS

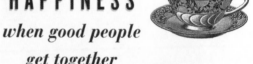

*when good people
get together*

Miss Bates, *Emma*

I have Loved None BUT YOU

Captain Wentworth, *Persuasion*

*Think only
of the past
as its remembrance
gives you*

PLEASURE

Elizabeth Bennet, *Pride and Prejudice*

Jane's Papers Ltd. is a paper goods company founded by devout
Janeite Darby Walker, in collaboration with Los Angeles–
based creative directors Elaine Suh Bartlett and Brad Bartlett.
Together, they create stationery that brings together classic
literature, art, and typography.

ISBN 978-1-4521-1330-2

Manufactured in China.

Design by Elaine Suh Bartlett and Brad Bartlett.

10 9 8 7 6 5 4 3 2

Find more Jane Austen gifts
at www.chroniclebooks.com.

CHRONICLE BOOKS
680 SECOND STREET
SAN FRANCISCO, CA 94107
WWW.CHRONICLEBOOKS.COM